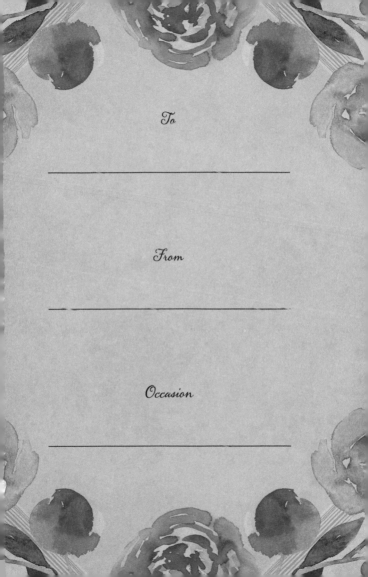

To

_____

From

_____

Occasion

_____

a bouquet of

Sweet Inspiration

to grow your faith

Tyndale House Publishers, Inc.

CAROL STREAM, ILLINOIS

Listen to me, O family of Jacob, Israel my chosen one! I alone am God, the First and the Last. It was my hand that laid the foundations of the earth, my right hand that spread out the heavens above. When I call out the stars, they all appear in order.

ISAIAH 48:12-13

I foretold the former
things long ago, my
mouth announced
them and I made
them known.

ISAIAH 48:3, NIV

In the image
of God has God
made mankind.

GENESIS 9:6, NIV

Christ is the visible image of the invisible God. He existed before anything was created and is supreme over all creation, for through him God created everything in the heavenly realms and on earth. He made the things we can see and the things we can't see. . . . Everything was created through him and for him. He existed before anything else, and he holds all creation together.

COLOSSIANS 1:15-17

"The time is coming," says the LORD, "when
I will raise up a righteous descendant from
King David's line. He will be a King who
rules with wisdom. He will do what is just
and right throughout the land."

JEREMIAH 23:5

I perceive him, but far
          in the distant future.
A star will rise from Jacob;
          a scepter will emerge
from Israel.

NUMBERS 24:17

Let us

EXAMINE

our ways and test
them, and let us return
to the LORD.

LAMENTATIONS 3:40, NIV

Come, let us return to the Lord. . . . In just a short time he will restore us, so that we may live in his presence. Oh, that we might know the Lord! Let us press on to know him. He will respond to us as surely as the arrival of dawn or the coming of rains in early spring.

HOSEA 6:1-3

The LORD says, "Turn to me now, while there is time. Give me your hearts. Come with fasting, weeping, and mourning. Don't tear your clothing in your grief, but tear your hearts instead." Return to the LORD your God, for he is merciful and compassionate, slow to get angry and filled with unfailing love. He is eager to relent and not punish.

JOEL 2:12-13

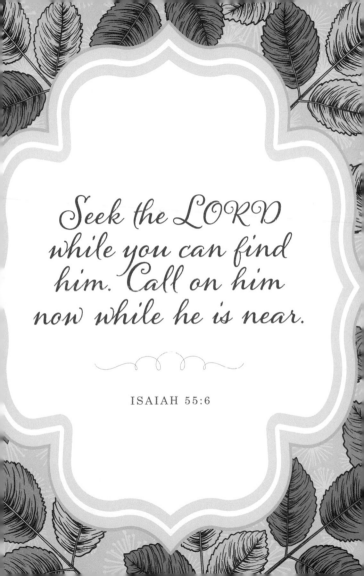

Seek the LORD while you can find him. Call on him now while he is near.

ISAIAH 55:6

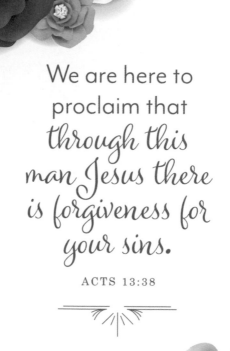

We are here to
proclaim that
*through this
man Jesus there
is forgiveness for
your sins.*

ACTS 13:38

Christ suffered for our sins once for all
time. He never sinned, but he died for
sinners to bring you safely home to God.
He suffered physical death, but he was
raised to life in the Spirit.

1 PETER 3:18

We are made right with God by placing our faith in Jesus Christ. And this is true for everyone who believes, no matter who we are. For everyone has sinned; we all fall short of God's glorious standard. Yet God, in his grace, freely makes us right in his sight. He did this through Christ Jesus when he freed us from the penalty for our sins.

ROMANS 3:22-24

Jesus said, "If you hold to my teaching . . . you will know the truth, and the truth will set you free."

JOHN 8:31-32, NIV

He saved us, not
because of the
righteous things
we had done, but
because of his mercy.

TITUS 3:5

Since we have been made right in God's sight
by faith, we have peace with God because
of what Jesus Christ our Lord has done for
us. Because of our faith, Christ has brought
us into this place of undeserved privilege
where we now stand, and we confidently and
joyfully look forward to sharing God's glory.

ROMANS 5:1-2

May God give
you more and
more mercy,
peace, and love.

JUDE 1:2

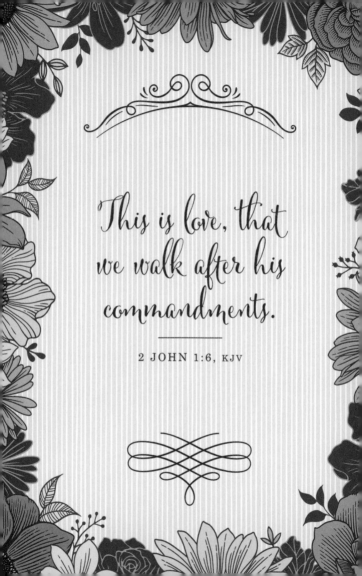

This is love, that
we walk after his
commandments.

2 JOHN 1:6, KJV

These commandments that I give you today
are to be on your hearts. Impress them on
your children. Talk about them when you sit
at home and when you walk along the road,
when you lie down and when you get up.

DEUTERONOMY 6:6-7, NIV

What does the LORD your God require of you?
He requires only that you fear the LORD
your God, and live in a way that pleases
him, and love him and serve him with all
your heart and soul. And you must always
obey the LORD's commands and decrees that
I am giving you today for your own good.

DEUTERONOMY 10:12-13

Seek the Kingdom of God
above all else,
and live righteously,
and he will give you
everything you need.

MATTHEW 6:33

Hold on to what is

GOOD,

reject every kind
of evil.

1 THESSALONIANS 5:21-22, NIV

May the God of peace make you holy in every way, and may your whole spirit and soul and body be kept blameless until our Lord Jesus Christ comes again. God will make this happen, for he who calls you is faithful.

1 THESSALONIANS 5:23-24

We can rejoice, too, when we run into
problems and trials, for we know that they
help us develop endurance. And endurance
develops strength of character, and
character strengthens our confident hope
of salvation. And this hope will not lead
to disappointment. For we know how dearly
God loves us, because he has given us the
Holy Spirit to fill our hearts with his love.

ROMANS 5:3-5

I, the LORD,
love justice. I hate
robbery and wrongdoing.
I will faithfully reward
my people for their
suffering.

ISAIAH 61:8

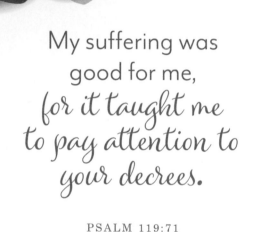

My suffering was
good for me,
for it taught me
to pay attention to
your decrees.

PSALM 119:71

Though I walk in the midst of trouble, you preserve my life; you stretch out your hand against the wrath of my enemies, and your right hand delivers me. The LORD will fulfill his purpose for me; your steadfast love, O LORD, endures forever. Do not forsake the work of your hands.

PSALM 138:7-8, ESV

My dear brothers and sisters, if someone
among you wanders away from the truth
and is brought back, you can be sure
that whoever brings the sinner back from
wandering will save that person from
death and bring about the forgiveness
of many sins.

JAMES 5:19-20

There will be more joy in heaven over one sinner who repents than over ninety-nine . . . who need no repentance.

LUKE 15:7, NKJV

The Sovereign LORD
says: I myself will
search for my sheep
and look after them.

EZEKIEL 34:11, NIV

I will say to the prisoners, "Come out in freedom," and to those in darkness, "Come into the light." They will be my sheep, grazing in green pastures and on hills that were previously bare. They will neither hunger nor thirst. The searing sun will not reach them anymore. For the LORD in his mercy will lead them; he will lead them beside cool waters.

ISAIAH 49:9-10

Those who trust
in the LORD
will lack no
good thing.

PSALM 34:10

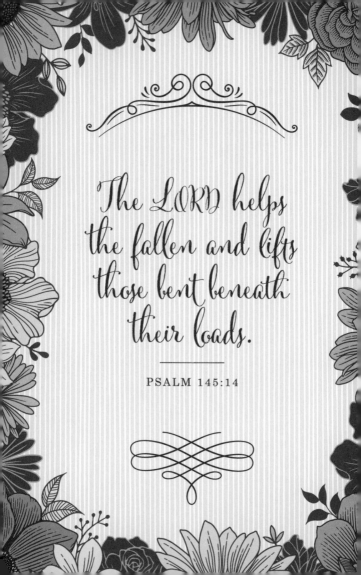

The LORD helps
the fallen and lifts
those bent beneath
their loads.

PSALM 145:14

When you give to someone in need, don't do
as the hypocrites do—blowing trumpets in
the synagogues and streets to call attention
to their acts of charity! . . . When you give
to someone in need, don't let your left hand
know what your right hand is doing. Give
your gifts in private, and your Father, who
sees everything, will reward you.

MATTHEW 6:2-4

It was necessary for [Jesus] to be made
in every respect like us, his brothers and
sisters, so that he could be our merciful
and faithful High Priest before God. Then he
could offer a sacrifice that would take away
the sins of the people. Since he himself has
gone through suffering and testing, he is
able to help us when we are being tested.

HEBREWS 2:17-18

By one offering He has
          perfected forever
those who are
          being sanctified.

HEBREWS 10:14, NKJV

Glory to God in

HIGHEST HEAVEN,

and peace on earth to
those with whom God
is pleased.

LUKE 2:14

God has made everything beautiful for its own time. He has planted eternity in the human heart, but even so, people cannot see the whole scope of God's work from beginning to end. So I concluded there is nothing better than to be happy and enjoy ourselves as long as we can. And people should eat and drink and enjoy the fruits of their labor, for these are gifts from God.

ECCLESIASTES 3:11-13

If your gift is serving others, serve them well. If you are a teacher, teach well. If your gift is to encourage others, be encouraging. If it is giving, give generously. If God has given you leadership ability, take the responsibility seriously. And if you have a gift for showing kindness to others, do it gladly.

ROMANS 12:7-8

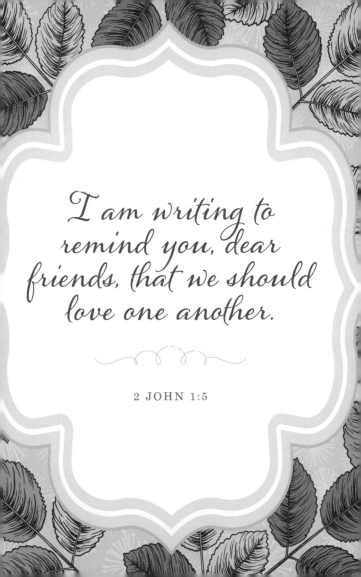

I am writing to remind you, dear friends, that we should love one another.

2 JOHN 1:5

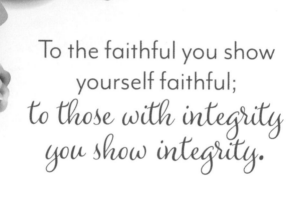

To the faithful you show
yourself faithful;
to those with integrity
you show integrity.

2 SAMUEL 22:26

The Lord is my rock, my fortress, and my savior; my God is my rock, in whom I find protection. He is my shield, the power that saves me, and my place of safety. He is my refuge, my savior, the one who saves me from violence. I called on the Lord, who is worthy of praise, and he saved me from my enemies.

2 SAMUEL 22:2-4

[The Lord] said to me, "My grace is sufficient for you, for my power is made perfect in weakness." Therefore I will boast all the more gladly of my weaknesses, so that the power of Christ may rest upon me. For the sake of Christ, then, I am content with weaknesses, insults, hardships, persecutions, and calamities. For when I am weak, then I am strong.

2 CORINTHIANS 12:9-10, ESV

The more we suffer for
Christ, the more God will
shower us with his comfort
through Christ.

2 CORINTHIANS 1:5

Jesus said,
"Come to me, all of
you who are weary
and carry heavy
burdens, and I will
give you rest."

A good tree can't produce bad fruit, and a bad tree can't produce good fruit. A tree is identified by its fruit. Figs are never gathered from thornbushes, and grapes are not picked from bramble bushes. A good person produces good things from the treasury of a good heart, and an evil person produces evil things from the treasury of an evil heart. What you say flows from what is in your heart.

LUKE 6:43-45

The LORD . . .
delights in those
whose ways are
blameless.

PROVERBS 11:20, NIV

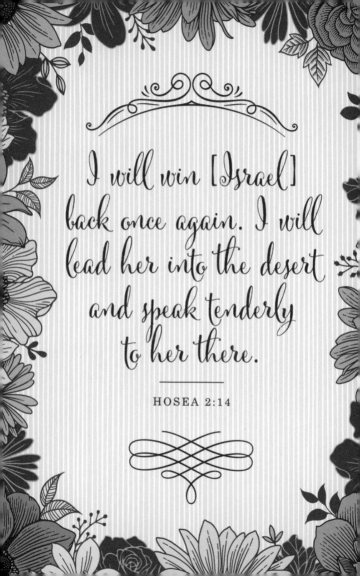

I will win [Israel] back once again. I will lead her into the desert and speak tenderly to her there.

HOSEA 2:14

The time will come when Israel's people will be like the sands of the seashore—too many to count! Then, at the place where they were told, "You are not my people," it will be said, "You are children of the living God." Then the people of Judah and Israel will unite together. They will choose one leader for themselves, and they will return from exile together. What a day that will be . . . when God will again plant his people in his land.

HOSEA 1:10-11

The LORD will have mercy on the descendants of Jacob. . . . He will bring them back to settle once again in their own land. And people from many different nations will come and join them there and unite with the people of Israel. The nations of the world will help the people of Israel to return, and those who come to live in the LORD's land will serve them.

ISAIAH 14:1-2

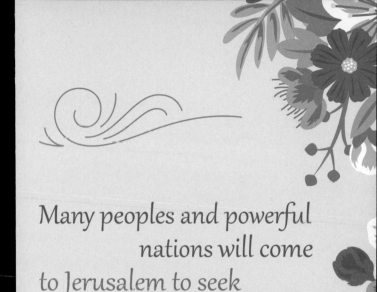

Many peoples and powerful
nations will come
to Jerusalem to seek
the LORD Almighty.

ZECHARIAH 8:20, NIV

There is

NO LONGER

Jew or Gentile, slave
or free, male or female.
For you are all one in
Christ Jesus.

GALATIANS 3:28

I am not ashamed of the gospel, because
it is the power of God that brings
salvation to everyone who believes: first
to the Jew, then to the Gentile. For in
the gospel the righteousness of God is
revealed—a righteousness that is by faith
from first to last, just as it is written:
"The righteous will live by faith."

ROMANS 1:16-17, NIV

How beautiful on the mountains are the feet of the messenger who brings good news, the good news of peace and salvation, the news that the God of Israel reigns! . . . The LORD has demonstrated his holy power before the eyes of all the nations. All the ends of the earth will see the victory of our God.

ISAIAH 52:7, 10

The Good News about the Kingdom will be preached throughout the whole world, so that all nations will hear it.

MATTHEW 24:14

Great are the works
of the LORD;
they are pondered
by all who delight
in them.

PSALM 111:2, NIV

Solomon stood before the altar of the LORD in front of the entire community of Israel. He lifted his hands toward heaven, and he prayed, "O LORD, God of Israel, there is no God like you in all of heaven above or on the earth below. You keep your covenant and show unfailing love to all who walk before you in wholehearted devotion."

1 KINGS 8:22-23

This is what the Lord says—Israel's King
and Redeemer, the Lord of Heaven's Armies:
"I am the First and the Last; there is no
other God. Who is like me? Let him step
forward and prove to you his power. . . .
You are my witnesses—is there any other
God? No! There is no other Rock—not one!"

ISAIAH 44:6-8

Trust in the LORD always,
for the LORD GOD is the
eternal Rock.

ISAIAH 26:4

The Rock! His work
is perfect, for all His
ways are just; a God
of faithfulness and
without injustice.

DEUTERONOMY 32:4, NASB

Have you not known? Have you not heard? The everlasting God, the LORD, the Creator of the ends of the earth, neither faints nor is weary. His understanding is unsearchable. He gives power to the weak, and to those who have no might He increases strength.

ISAIAH 40:28-29, NKJV

The joy of the LORD
is your strength.

NEHEMIAH 8:10, KJV

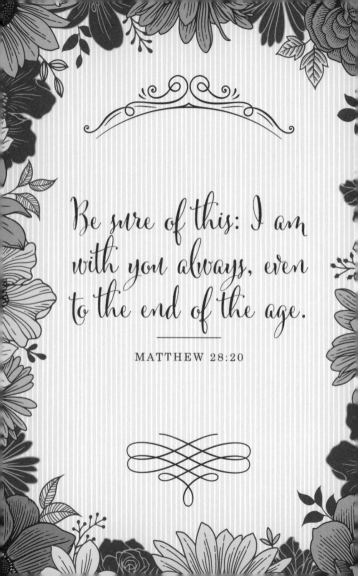

Be sure of this: I am
with you always, even
to the end of the age.

MATTHEW 28:20

What can we bring to the LORD? Should
we bring him burnt offerings? . . . Should
we offer him thousands of rams and
ten thousand rivers of olive oil? . . .
No, O people, the LORD has told you what
is good, and this is what he requires of
you: to do what is right, to love mercy,
and to walk humbly with your God.

MICAH 6:6-8

A child is born to us, a son is given to us.
The government will rest on his shoulders.
And he will be called: Wonderful Counselor,
Mighty God, Everlasting Father, Prince of
Peace. His government and its peace will
never end. He will rule with fairness and
justice from the throne of his ancestor
David for all eternity.

ISAIAH 9:6-7

Let justice roll
        on like a river,
righteousness like a
    never-failing stream!

AMOS 5:24, NIV

Do not be

CONFORMED

to this world, but be
transformed by the
renewing of your mind.

ROMANS 12:2, NKJV

Whatsoever things are true, whatsoever things are honest, whatsoever things are just, whatsoever things are pure, whatsoever things are lovely, whatsoever things are of good report; if there be any virtue, and if there be any praise, think on these things. Those things, which ye have both learned, and received, and heard, and seen in me, do: and the God of peace shall be with you.

PHILIPPIANS 4:8-9, KJV

The LORD spoke to Moses, saying, "Speak to Aaron and his sons, saying, Thus you shall bless the people of Israel: you shall say to them, The LORD bless you and keep you; the LORD make his face to shine upon you and be gracious to you; the LORD lift up his countenance upon you and give you peace."

NUMBERS 6:22-26, ESV

The LORD
is gracious and
compassionate, slow
to anger and rich
in love.

PSALM 145:8, NIV

The LORD is good, a strong refuge when trouble comes. He is close to those who trust in him.

NAHUM 1:7

Be strong in the Lord and in his mighty power. Put on all of God's armor so that you will be able to stand firm against all strategies of the devil. For we are not fighting against flesh-and-blood enemies, but against evil rulers and authorities of the unseen world, against mighty powers in this dark world, and against evil spirits in the heavenly places.

EPHESIANS 6:10-12

Stand your ground, putting on the belt
of truth and the body armor of God's
righteousness. For shoes, put on the peace
that comes from the Good News so that
you will be fully prepared. . . . Hold up the
shield of faith to stop the fiery arrows of
the devil. Put on salvation as your helmet,
and take the sword of the Spirit, which is
the word of God.

EPHESIANS 6:14-17

The LORD is my strength
and my song, and he has
become my salvation.

EXODUS 15:2, ESV

He who dwells
in the secret place
of the Most High
shall abide under
the shadow of the
Almighty.

PSALM 91:1, NKJV

Make it your goal to live a quiet life, minding your own business and working with your hands, just as we instructed you before. Then people who are not believers will respect the way you live, and you will not need to depend on others.

1 THESSALONIANS 4:11-12

Live wisely among
those who are
not believers, and
make the most of
every opportunity.

COLOSSIANS 4:5

Let us not grow weary
while doing good,
for in due season we
shall reap if we do
not lose heart.

GALATIANS 6:9, NKJV

Even youths will become weak and tired, and young men will fall in exhaustion. But those who trust in the LORD will find new strength. They will soar high on wings like eagles. They will run and not grow weary. They will walk and not faint.

ISAIAH 40:30-31

The LORD says, . . . "I am the one who
answers your prayers and cares for you.
I am like a tree that is always green; all
your fruit comes from me." Let those who are
wise understand these things. Let those with
discernment listen carefully. The paths of
the LORD are true and right, and righteous
people live by walking in them.

HOSEA 14:4, 8-9

Rejoice always,
    pray continually,
give thanks in
    all circumstances;
for this is God's will
    for you.

1 THESSALONIANS 5:16-18, NIV

Don't worry about

TOMORROW,

for tomorrow will
bring its own worries.
Today's trouble is
enough for today.

MATTHEW 6:34

Do not be afraid, for I have ransomed you.
I have called you by name; you are mine.
When you go through deep waters, I will be
with you. When you go through rivers of
difficulty, you will not drown. . . . For I am
the LORD, your God, the Holy One of Israel,
your Savior.

ISAIAH 43.1-3

Make every effort to add to your faith goodness; and to goodness, knowledge; and to knowledge, self-control; and to self-control, perseverance; and to perseverance, godliness; and to godliness, mutual affection; and to mutual affection, love. For if you possess these qualities in increasing measure, they will keep you from being ineffective and unproductive in your knowledge of our Lord Jesus Christ.

2 PETER 1:5-8, NIV

Faith comes from hearing, that is, hearing the Good News about Christ.

ROMANS 10:17

We are God's handiwork, created in Christ Jesus to do good works.

EPHESIANS 2:10, NIV

All Scripture is inspired by God and is useful to teach us what is true and to make us realize what is wrong in our lives. It corrects us when we are wrong and teaches us to do what is right. God uses it to prepare and equip his people to do every good work.

2 TIMOTHY 3:16-17

The word of God is alive and powerful. It is sharper than the sharpest two-edged sword, cutting between soul and spirit, between joint and marrow. It exposes our innermost thoughts and desires. Nothing in all creation is hidden from God. Everything is naked and exposed before his eyes, and he is the one to whom we are accountable.

HEBREWS 4:12-13

The eyes of the LORD
range throughout the
earth to strengthen those
whose hearts are fully
committed to him.

2 CHRONICLES 16:9, NIV

*As for me
and my house,
we will serve
the LORD.*

JOSHUA 24:15, NKJV

Free those who are wrongly imprisoned;
lighten the burden of those who work for
you. Let the oppressed go free, and remove
the chains that bind people. Share your food
with the hungry, and give shelter to the
homeless. Give clothes to those who need
them, and do not hide from relatives who
need your help. Then your salvation will
come like the dawn.

ISAIAH 58:6-8

Faith by itself,
if it does not
have works,
is dead.

JAMES 2:17, NKJV

I will forgive their wickedness, and I will never again remember their sins.

HEBREWS 8:12

Let the wicked change their ways and banish the very thought of doing wrong. Let them turn to the LORD that he may have mercy on them. Yes, turn to our God, for he will forgive generously. "My thoughts are nothing like your thoughts," says the LORD. "And my ways are far beyond anything you could imagine."

ISAIAH 55:7-9

You must worship Christ as Lord of your life. And if someone asks about your hope as a believer, always be ready to explain it. But do this in a gentle and respectful way. Keep your conscience clear. Then if people speak against you, they will be ashamed when they see what a good life you live because you belong to Christ.

1 PETER 3:15-16

Do not imitate what
is evil but what is good.
Anyone who does what
is good is from God.

3 JOHN 1:11, NIV

Pray in the

SPIRIT

at all times. . . .
Stay alert and be
persistent in your prayers
for all believers.

EPHESIANS 6:18

We are confident that he hears us whenever
we ask for anything that pleases him. And
since we know he hears us when we make
our requests, we also know that he will give
us what we ask for.

1 JOHN 5:14-15

I am convinced that neither death nor
life, neither angels nor demons, neither the
present nor the future, nor any powers,
neither height nor depth, nor anything else
in all creation, will be able to separate us
from the love of God that is in Christ Jesus
our Lord.

ROMANS 8:38-39, NIV

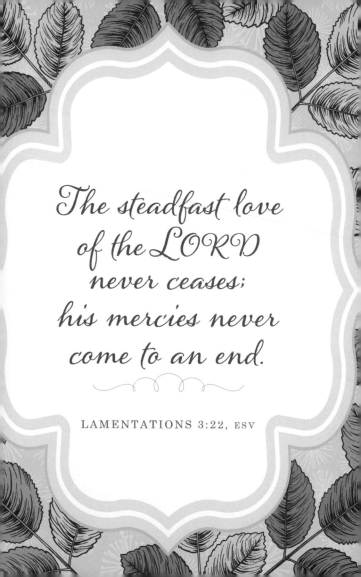

The steadfast love
of the LORD
never ceases;
his mercies never
come to an end.

LAMENTATIONS 3:22, ESV

You yourselves are
*taught by God to love
one another.*

1 THESSALONIANS 4:9, NKJV

Above all, clothe yourselves with love, which binds us all together in perfect harmony. And let the peace that comes from Christ rule in your hearts. For as members of one body you are called to live in peace. And always be thankful. Let the message about Christ, in all its richness, fill your lives.

COLOSSIANS 3:14-16

Understand, therefore, that the LORD your God is indeed God. He is the faithful God who keeps his covenant for a thousand generations and lavishes his unfailing love on those who love him and obey his commands.

DEUTERONOMY 7:9

He has given us this command: Anyone who loves God must also love their brother and sister.

1 JOHN 4:21, NIV

We know,
brothers and
sisters loved by
god, that he has

chosen you.

1 THESSALONIANS 1:4, NIV

Let each of you look not only to his own interests, but also to the interests of others. Have this mind among yourselves, which is yours in Christ Jesus, who, though he was in the form of God, did not count equality with God a thing to be grasped, but emptied himself, by taking the form of a servant, being born in the likeness of men.

PHILIPPIANS 2:4-7, ESV

Let's not merely say that we love each other; let us show the truth by our actions.

1 JOHN 3:18

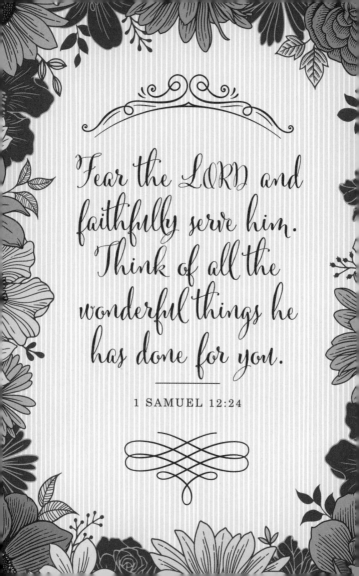

Fear the LORD and faithfully serve him. Think of all the wonderful things he has done for you.

1 SAMUEL 12:24

Work hard so you can present yourself
to God and receive his approval. Be a
good worker, one who does not need to be
ashamed and who correctly explains the
word of truth. Avoid worthless, foolish talk
that only leads to more godless behavior.

2 TIMOTHY 2:15-16

Look! I stand at the door and knock. If
you hear my voice and open the door, I will
come in, and we will share a meal together
as friends. Those who are victorious will
sit with me on my throne, just as I was
victorious and sat with my Father on
his throne.

REVELATION 3:20-21

The grace of God
has been revealed,
bringing salvation
to all people.

TITUS 2:11

Arise, shine, for your

LIGHT

has come, and the glory of the LORD rises upon you.

ISAIAH 60:1, NIV

In the beginning was the Word, and the Word was with God, and the Word was God. He was with God in the beginning. Through him all things were made; without him nothing was made that has been made. In him was life, and that life was the light of all mankind. The light shines in the darkness, and the darkness has not overcome it.

JOHN 1:1-5, NIV

God is so rich in mercy, and he loved us so much, that even though we were dead because of our sins, he gave us life when he raised Christ from the dead. (It is only by God's grace that you have been saved!) For he raised us from the dead along with Christ and seated us with him in the heavenly realms because we are united with Christ Jesus.

EPHESIANS 2:4-6

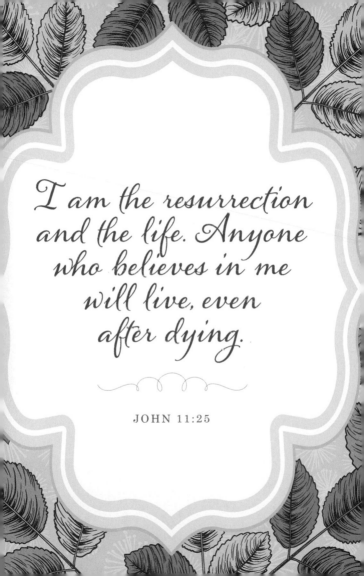

I am the resurrection
and the life. Anyone
who believes in me
will live, even
after dying.

JOHN 11:25

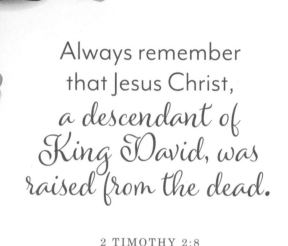

Always remember
that Jesus Christ,
a descendant of
King David, was
raised from the dead.

2 TIMOTHY 2:8

The Son is the radiance of God's glory
and the exact representation of his being,
sustaining all things by his powerful word.
After he had provided purification for
sins, he sat down at the right hand of the
Majesty in heaven.

HEBREWS 1:3, NIV

I press on to possess that perfection for
which Christ Jesus first possessed me.
No, dear brothers and sisters, I have not
achieved it, but I focus on this one thing:
Forgetting the past and looking forward to
what lies ahead, I press on to reach the
end of the race and receive the heavenly
prize for which God, through Christ Jesus,
is calling us.

PHILIPPIANS 3:12-14

To me to live is Christ,
and to die is gain.

PHILIPPIANS 1:21, KJV

If you cling to your life, you will lose it; but if you give up your life for me, you **will find it.**

MATTHEW 10:39

How great are God's riches and wisdom and knowledge! How impossible it is for us to understand his decisions and his ways! . . . Who knows enough to give him advice? And who has given him so much that he needs to pay it back? For everything comes from him and exists by his power and is intended for his glory.

ROMANS 11:33-36

I am the LORD,
the God of all
the peoples of the
world. Is anything
too hard for me?

JEREMIAH 32:27

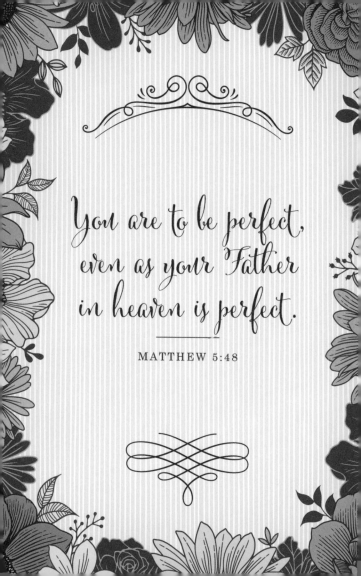

You are to be perfect,
even as your Father
in heaven is perfect.

MATTHEW 5:48

Dear brothers and sisters, when troubles
of any kind come your way, consider it an
opportunity for great joy. For you know that
when your faith is tested, your endurance
has a chance to grow. So let it grow, for
when your endurance is fully developed,
you will be perfect and complete, needing
nothing.

JAMES 1:2-4

The LORD your God is living among you. He is a mighty savior. He will take delight in you with gladness. With his love, he will calm all your fears. He will rejoice over you with joyful songs.

ZEPHANIAH 3:17

I sought the LORD,
and he heard me,
and delivered me
from all my fears.

PSALM 34:4, KJV

Store your

TREASURES

in heaven, where
moths and rust cannot
destroy, and thieves do
not break in and steal.

MATTHEW 6:20

Love your enemies! Do good to them. Lend to them without expecting to be repaid. Then your reward from heaven will be very great, and you will truly be acting as children of the Most High, for he is kind to those who are unthankful and wicked. You must be compassionate, just as your Father is compassionate.

LUKE 6:35-36

Remember, dear brothers and sisters, that few of you were wise in the world's eyes or powerful or wealthy when God called you. Instead, God chose things the world considers foolish in order to shame those who think they are wise. And he chose things that are powerless to shame those who are powerful.

1 CORINTHIANS 1:26-27

God opposes the
proud but gives
grace to the humble.

JAMES 4:6

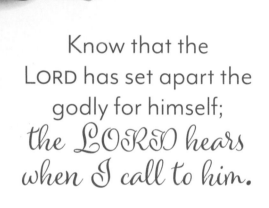

Know that the
LORD has set apart the
godly for himself;
the LORD hears
when I call to him.

PSALM 4:3, ESV

My old self has been crucified with Christ.
It is no longer I who live, but Christ lives
in me. So I live in this earthly body by
trusting in the Son of God, who loved me
and gave himself for me.

GALATIANS 2:20

Don't you realize that your body is the temple of the Holy Spirit, who lives in you and was given to you by God? You do not belong to yourself, for God bought you with a high price. So you must honor God with your body.

1 CORINTHIANS 6:19-20

God's temple is holy,
and you are that temple.

1 CORINTHIANS 3:17

The LORD is in his holy Temple. Let all the earth be silent before him.

HABAKKUK 2:20

Those who wish to boast should boast
in this alone: that they truly know me
and understand that I am the LORD who
demonstrates unfailing love and who brings
justice and righteousness to the earth, and
that I delight in these things. I, the LORD,
have spoken!

JEREMIAH 9:24

Give thanks to the
LORD, for he is good!
His faithful love
endures forever.

PSALM 118:1

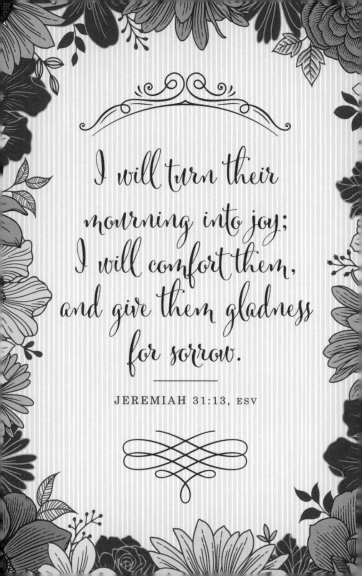

I will turn their
mourning into joy;
I will comfort them,
and give them gladness
for sorrow.

JEREMIAH 31:13, ESV

The LORD says: "Sing with joy for Israel. Shout for the greatest of nations! . . . For I will bring them from the north and from the distant corners of the earth. . . . A great company will return! Tears of joy will stream down their faces, and I will lead them home with great care. They will walk beside quiet streams and on smooth paths where they will not stumble."

JEREMIAH 31:7-9

We are citizens of heaven, where the Lord Jesus Christ lives. And we are eagerly waiting for him to return as our Savior. He will take our weak mortal bodies and change them into glorious bodies like his own, using the same power with which he will bring everything under his control.

PHILIPPIANS 3:20-21

We will all be transformed!
It will happen . . .
in the blink of an eye, when
the last trumpet is blown.

1 CORINTHIANS 15:51-52

He is the living

GOD,

and he will endure
forever. His kingdom
will never be destroyed.

DANIEL 6:26

The one sitting on the throne said, "Look, I am making everything new! . . . I am the Alpha and the Omega—the Beginning and the End. To all who are thirsty I will give freely from the springs of the water of life. All who are victorious will inherit all these blessings, and I will be their God, and they will be my children."

REVELATION 21:5-7

To him who loves us and has freed us from our sins by his blood, and has made us to be a kingdom and priests to serve his God and Father—to him be glory and power for ever and ever! Amen.

REVELATION 1:5-6, NIV

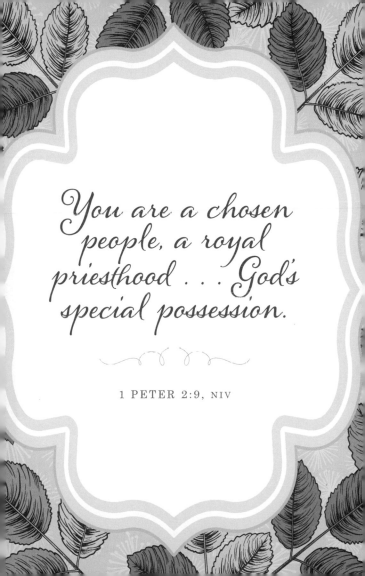

You are a chosen
people, a royal
priesthood . . . God's
special possession.

1 PETER 2:9, NIV

Let everyone see that you are
considerate in all you do.
*Remember, the Lord
is coming soon.*

PHILIPPIANS 4:5

The angel showed me a river with the water of life, clear as crystal. . . . On each side of the river grew a tree of life. . . . No longer will there be a curse upon anything. For the throne of God and of the Lamb will be there, and his servants will worship him. . . . And they will reign forever and ever. . . . He who is the faithful witness to all these things says, "Yes, I am coming soon!" Amen! Come, Lord Jesus!

REVELATION 22:1-3, 5, 20

LIVING
EXPRESSIONS
COLLECTION

Living Expressions invites you to explore God's Word
and express your creativity in ways that are refreshing
to the spirit and restorative to the soul.

Visit Tyndale online at www.tyndale.com.

TYNDALE, Tyndale's quill logo, *Living Expressions*, and the Living Expressions logo
are registered trademarks of Tyndale House Publishers, Inc.

A Bouquet of Sweet Inspiration to Grow Your Faith

For information about special discounts for bulk purchases, please contact Tyndale
House Publishers at csresponse@tyndale.com, or call 1-800-323-9400.

ISBN 978-1-4964-3606-1

Printed in China